# This book belongs to:

_____

_____

This is a work of fiction. Any resemblance to actual persons, living or dead, events or locales is entirely coincidental.

Text and Illustrations Copyright © Dave Whittle 2023

All songs Copyright © Dave Whittle 2023 and published by Maori Music 2023

Illustrations by Kris Lillyman 2023

Moral rights asserted

The right of Dave Whittle and Kris Lillyman to be identified as the Author and Illustrator of this work has been asserted by them in accordance with the Copyright, Design and Patents Act 1988.

All rights reserved. No part of this publication may be reproduced, stored in a retrieval system, or transmitted, in any form, or by any means (electronic, mechanical, photocopying, recording or otherwise) without the prior written permission of the publisher.

# Pirates Rule Okay!
## Songbook

Dave Whittle

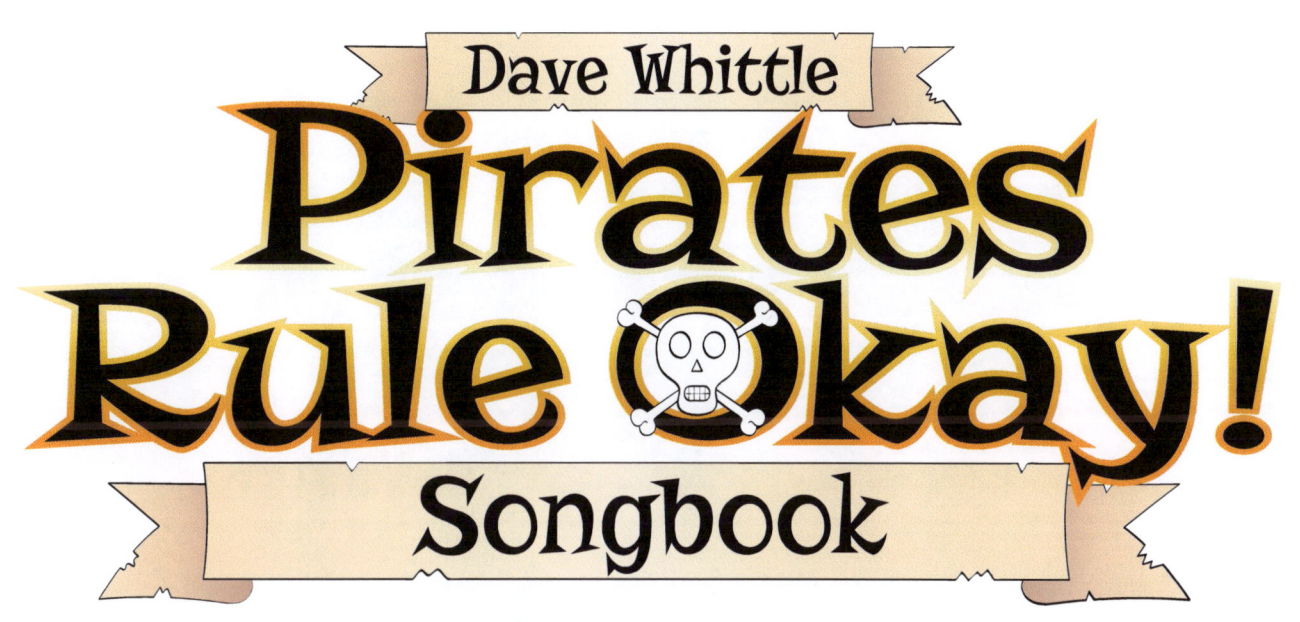

Illustrated by Kris Lillyman

Welcome to the world of Captain Barnabas Bligh and his very own golden age of piracy!

Famous for trading with smugglers and plundering booty from naval ships out on the high seas, he is joined by a loyal and brave rag-tag crew.

They all have a very hard time avoiding capture by members of His Majesty's coastguard service.

# PIRATES RULE OKAY!

**WANTED FOR PIRACY**
CAP'N BARNABAS BLIGH
REWARD

YE OLDE PAINT

Now let us hear, in song and verse, a rollicking adventure of love at sea and a hunt for buried treasure!

# Pirate Ladies

In a Cornish cove, on golden sand, a group of hard-working women folk sing about who they really are.

### Chorus

Pirate ladies are we
Pirate ladies are we
Pirate ladies are we....

We are the girls who venture out to sea
The daughters of the British nobility
Villainy, oh piracy
Rule our lives just like the pirate men
Let's sing again....

### Chorus

It's said we are the pretty girls of crime
But we remember when there was a time
Of honesty, oh loyalty
Ruled our lives and bored us all to death
Take another breath....

### Chorus

If we had not changed to sailing cross the waves
At home we'd be just like those women slaves
Purgatory! No, not for me!
We earn a handsome wage that we deserve
We've got the nerve....

### Chorus

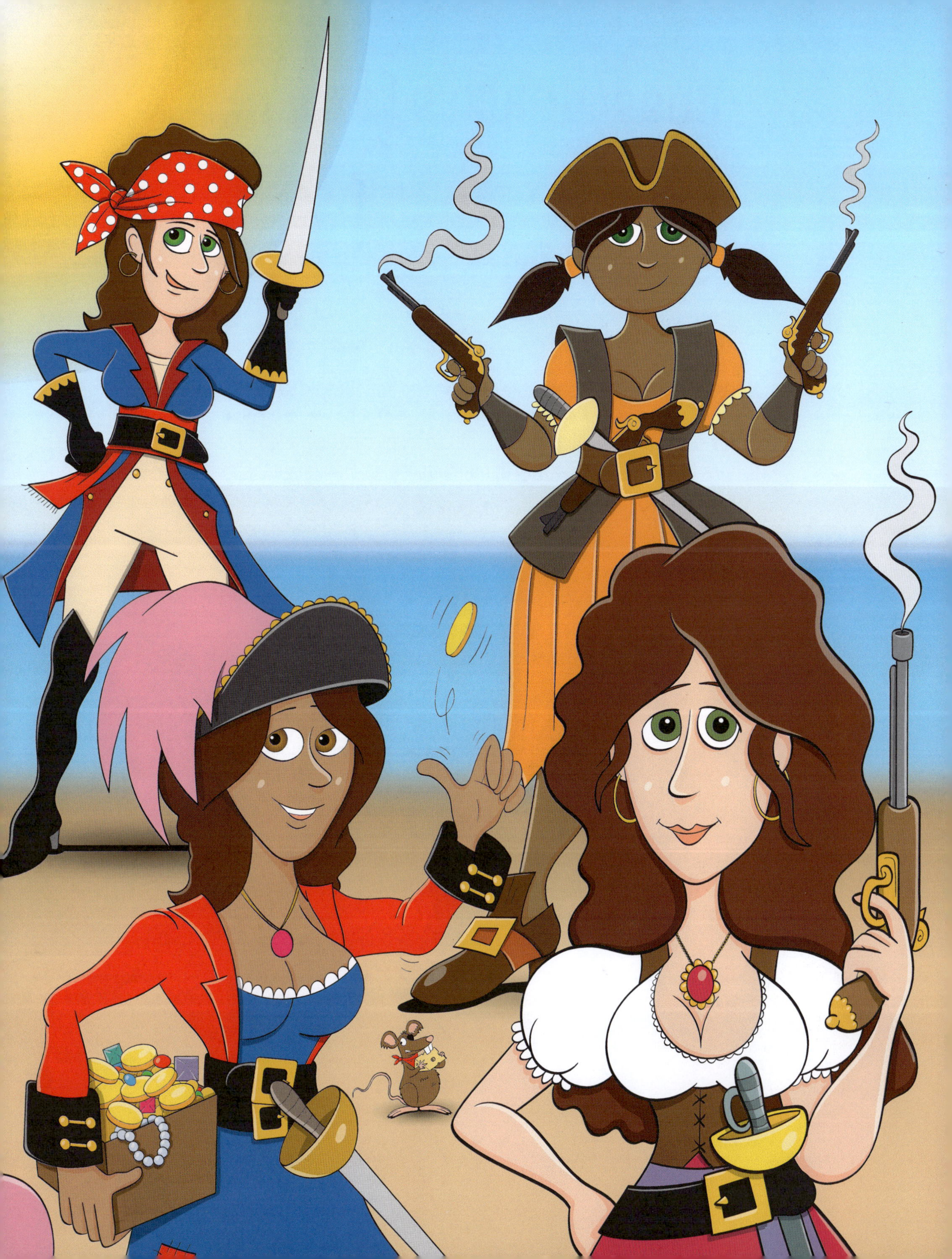

# Coastguard's Lament

Outside their clifftop hideout, the coastguards go about their daily business, looking out to sea for any pirates or smugglers.
Sergeant Rob, Constable Evans and Constable Crab are busy moaning about the British weather.

"We're the coastguards.... pirates and smugglers beware!"

We're employed in honourable duty by the honourable Scotland Yard
We are the law of the country and on clifftops we're on guard
For suspicious-looking gentlemen who carry out smuggling acts
Us poor old lonely policemen in our waterproof coastguard macs....

Chorus

We're the force of good old England
We work with our own bare hands
And if we should (if we should) if we should (if we should)
See a pirate band
We'll protect all the children of the land

When our feet are growing colder, while in stormy weather stood
We'll carry out our duty in our uniform of mud
By the end of the day, we look like washed-out sewer rats
Us poor old lonely policemen, in our waterproof coastguard hats....

Chorus

So, before you join the force young man, you'd better think some more
The problems we encounter when we represent the law
We can't make friends with cut-throats, or those crafty smuggling folk
"Who'd wanna make friends with cut-throats or 'em crafty smugglin' folk anyway, eh?"
"Indeed sir, no, no, absolutely not!"
Perhaps it's for the best we wear the waterproof coastguard cloak....

Chorus

Sergeant Rob

Constable Evans

Constable Crab

# Captain Bligh

Captain Bligh was traded a treasure map by crafty, old
Smuggler Sam, in return for some of the booty. Sam also insisted Bligh must keep
his side of the bargain, otherwise he would reveal a secret about Bligh,
that no-one else knows.

Bligh gathers up his crew for a good old singsong!

A merry band of pirates we
Outlawed by the aristocracy
Forever pirates we shall be
And I'm the cap'n.... yes that's me!

For I am Cap'n Bligh
Yes, he is Cap'n Bligh!
And I's only got one eye...
When I was a lad, I do decree
A wish I had to go to sea
When I grew up I became a deckhand
On a pirate ship, of a pirate band

For I am Cap'n Bligh
Yes, he is Cap'n Bligh!
And I never, ever cry
"What, never?"
"No, never!"
"What, never?"
"Well, hardly ever..."

I spent my time and I learnt my trade
Until at last I made the grade
A first-class rogue among rogues-a-few
So, I became...the cap'n of the crew

For I am Cap'n Bligh
Yes, he is Cap'n Bligh
And I's only got one eye

So now I've sailed the seven seas, my fame's
renowned everyone agrees
(His fame's renowned, everyone agrees!)
And all my mates, I'm proud to own
They never spit and they never moan
(We never spit and we never moan)

'Twas Rowena who was captured thus
She made no cry and she made no fuss
By a coastguard gang, I'd swear just here
They questioned her, about her career...

**OH HORROR!**
For Rowena was a pirate true
What on Earth are we going to do?

On a clifftop path their hideout stands
Five hundred feet 'bove golden sands
We must strike fast afore she speaks
They mustn't find out...else us they'll seek

So, we shall have to rescue her
'Twill be a deed of brave and terrible dare
An operation for one so sly...
ha ha ha haaa!
It's just the job... for Cap'n Bligh

For I am Cap'n Bligh
Yes, he is Cap'n Bligh!
And the pirate flag I fly...
Captain Bligh, Captain Bligh,
Captain Bligh!!

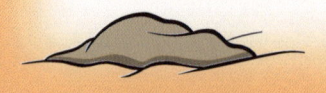

The piratical choir is disturbed by a worried pirate lady Bets, who informs that her twin sister, Rowena, has been captured by the coastguards and is now locked up in their clifftop gaol!

# Together (A Love Song)

Rowena is clever and hatches a plan to escape from her dungeon, by pointing out to the coastguards that they would be better off if they joined the pirates in search of treasure.

The pirates, who were attempting a rescue, are surprised to see Rowena free from her chains, as well as finding out that they have some new, unexpected, partners in crime!

Captain Barnabas is very impressed with Rowena's cunning deeds and invites her into his cabin, where they chat and giggle.

Love is very much in the air tonight.

If I had a wish, then she would be mine
If he had a wish, I'm sure it would be fine
But why don't all my dreams come true
I know that I belong with you

Chorus

Together, we want to be together
Your company forever
Yes ever, evermore
Together, we'll always be together
In harmony forever
'Cause you're the one I adore...

If I had a wish, then I'd ask for her
If he had his wish, I'd hope he'd really care
But why must my heart be made to ache
What a wonderful companion I'd make

Chorus

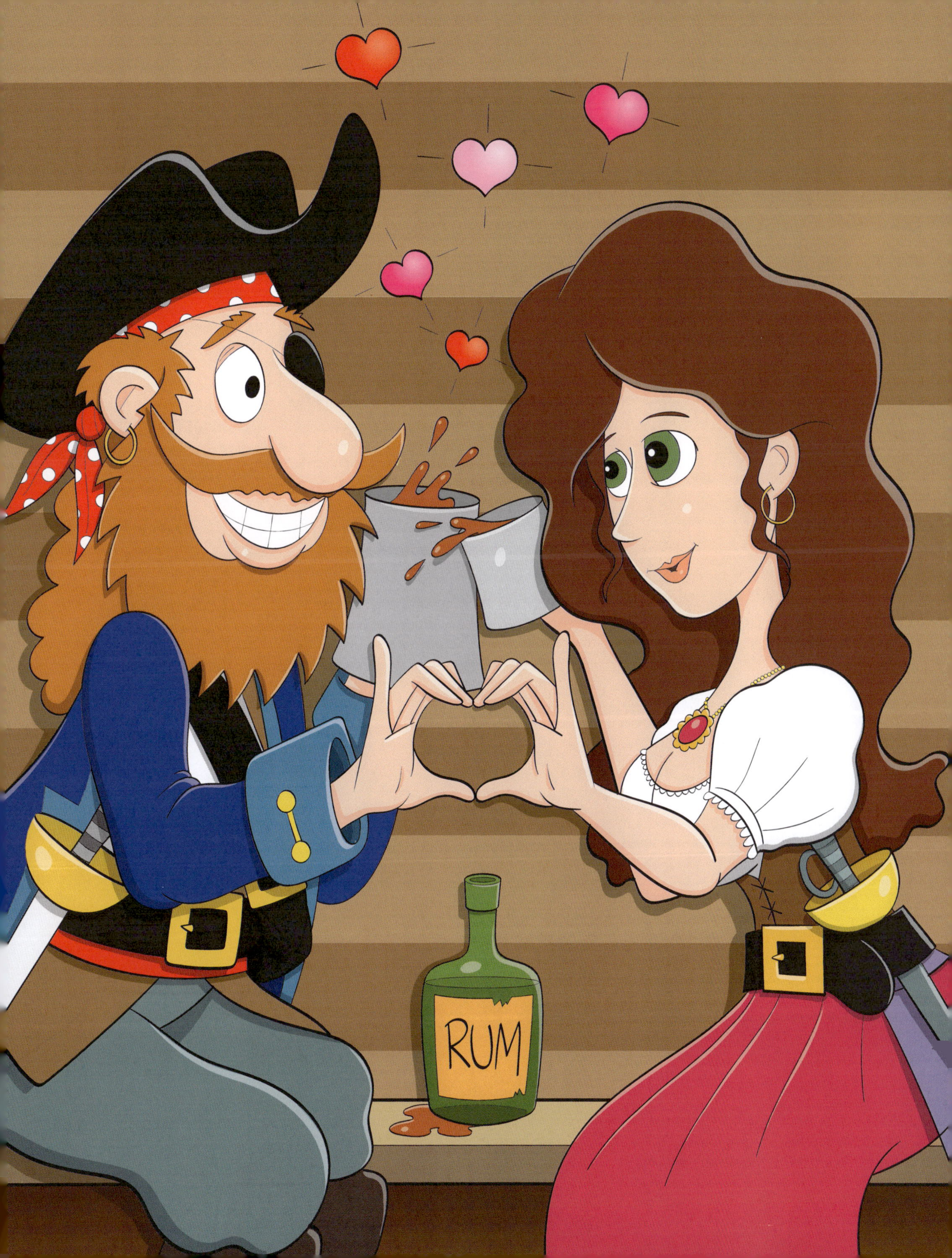
RUM

# Yo Ho Me Lads!

Captain Bligh tells his crew about the treasure map he has acquired, and they are all very eager to go on a treasure hunt.

PIRATICAL PETS
PURVEYORS OF THE FINEST PARROTS

THE BLACK SPOT
Fashion For Stylish Lads & Lassies

CRANIUM COVE

PALM ISLAND

Pirate Peaks

SHARKS!

Cut Throat Caves

Dead Man Falls

Mermaid Lagoon

Octopus Pass

Fi... Mou...

WHALE BAY

TREASURE

Crocodile Creek

Strange Statues

Mayan Ruins

ROUGH SEAS

Yo ho me lads, heave ho
There's treasure we must go

Yo ho me lads, heave ho
To the treasure we shall go!

Yo ho me lads, heave ho
There's treasure we must go

Yo ho me lads, heave ho
To the treasure we must go!

# Leader Of Us All

'Tis late in the evening and in a tavern down by the harbour, the newly formed crew eat well, make merry and sing the praises of their esteemed leader, Captain Barnabas Bligh!

When the bosun's caught a-nappin' and the sails they are a-flappin'
And our boat be driftin' off and off away
We call for our cap'n loudly and salute him, oh so proudly
When, once again, he goes and 'saves the day' ('saves the day')

Chorus

Brave is he, bold and ever-daring
Brings us all along, to enjoy the lovely view
We know what it's like when he wants to go a-rovin'
He's leader of us all you know and we're his motley crew
And we're his motley crew!

When the ship runs out of rum
And we're feelin' mighty glum
There be naught so fraught 'til we dock into port!
Yet 'tis our only duty, to but skirmish for our booty
Then we sail away before we e'er get caught (e'er get caught)

### Chorus

When there ain't so much as a carrot
We're as sick as a pirate's parrot
We're so 'ungry that we don't know what to do
We're at risk o' gettin' scurvy but our cap'n thinks us worthy
Cause he boils his socks and makes a tasty stew (tasty stew)

### Chorus

If we falls into 'the drink' and before we starts to sink
He might spy a 'shiver of sharks', come swimmin' by
And our cap'n dives right in, with his cutlass 'neath his chin
To the rescue afore he even starts to think (starts to think)

### Chorus

His motley, motley crew!

# The Pirate Ship's In Harbour

At dawn's first light, *The Salty Dog* is a-floatin' in the harbour and the crew are busy a-loadin' on board all the cargo provisions necessary to survive a perilous journey across the wild Atlantic Ocean.

Nevertheless, spirits are high, as they start to imagine the treasure that is said to be buried on a faraway desert island!

Come sail your ship and take a trip on the big blue briny waves
And for your pleasure but at your leisure, search for the treasure caves
Near Staghorn Crag, you should fly your flag, so we'll see the skull and crossbones
Here you'll hear, the moans and groans, from the 'Locker of Davy Jones'
(From the 'Locker of Davy Jones')

### Chorus

ALL ABOARD! (All aboard)
For the pirate ship's in harbour
ALL ABOARD! (All aboard)
She's a-sailin' come the dawn
ALL ABOARD! (All aboard)
For the pirate ship's in harbour
She'll sail away through skies a-grey, with a pirate's cutlass drawn
With a pirate's cutlass drawn....

Now without fail, take down your sail and keep your boat afloat
But don't flight until the night and you spy Cap'n Bligh, the cut-throat
He'll give you a sign at the stroke o' nine, to smuggle your wine ashore
And if a coastguard's there, don't despair...'twill be a pirate in disguise for sure!
('Twill be a pirate in disguise for sure)

### Chorus

Cap'n Blackbeard's endeared to swiggin' rum, or at least some other kind o' drink
And if you walk the plank, you've yourself to thank, he's no pity for those who sink
But we'll still go forth, head toward the north and plunder what comes by
Cause we're the crew, who never rue and never wonder why (no, never wonder why!)

### Chorus

The Bilge Rat & Barnacle
The Bilge Rat & Barnacle
ALE & GRUB
Something Fishy
The Salty Dog

# Jolly Roger

The ship has some pets: Squawk, a seagull who chats to Captain Bligh, Rufus the friendly terrier dog and Hilary the black cat, who is good at seeking out any unwelcome rodent passengers!

To while away time out at sea, the crew sing some well-known rib-ticklin' tales, whilst also paying homage to their fearsome flag, the Jolly Roger.

The bosun entertains, by doing a jig and playing his fiddle.

"Now let's hear about some of 'em wild, seafaring tales"

My father was a sailor, he sailed the seven seas
But he suffered from an illness, that made him always sneeze
So, he carried a store of hankies, to wipe his big fat nose
And when he put one to his face, they all cried "thar she blows"

Chorus

Jolly, Jolly Roger,
Flying in the breeze
Hail to the pirate flag flying high
O'er the great blue briny seas...

"Rowena, what about that one about Agnes?"

Now Agnes was a milkmaid, she tended to the cows
She had an awful temper and she entered many rows
But one day while a-milking, she shouted at the beast
The cow jumped up right on top of her and now she is deceased!

Chorus

"And then there was that one about poor old Charlie..."

Now Charlie, he was an angel, the nicest of them all
He flew across the sky, he did and he blew the trumpet call
To summon all the angels, by giving the battle cry
For the Devil himself was a-comin'... it was good ol' Cap'n Bligh!!

Chorus

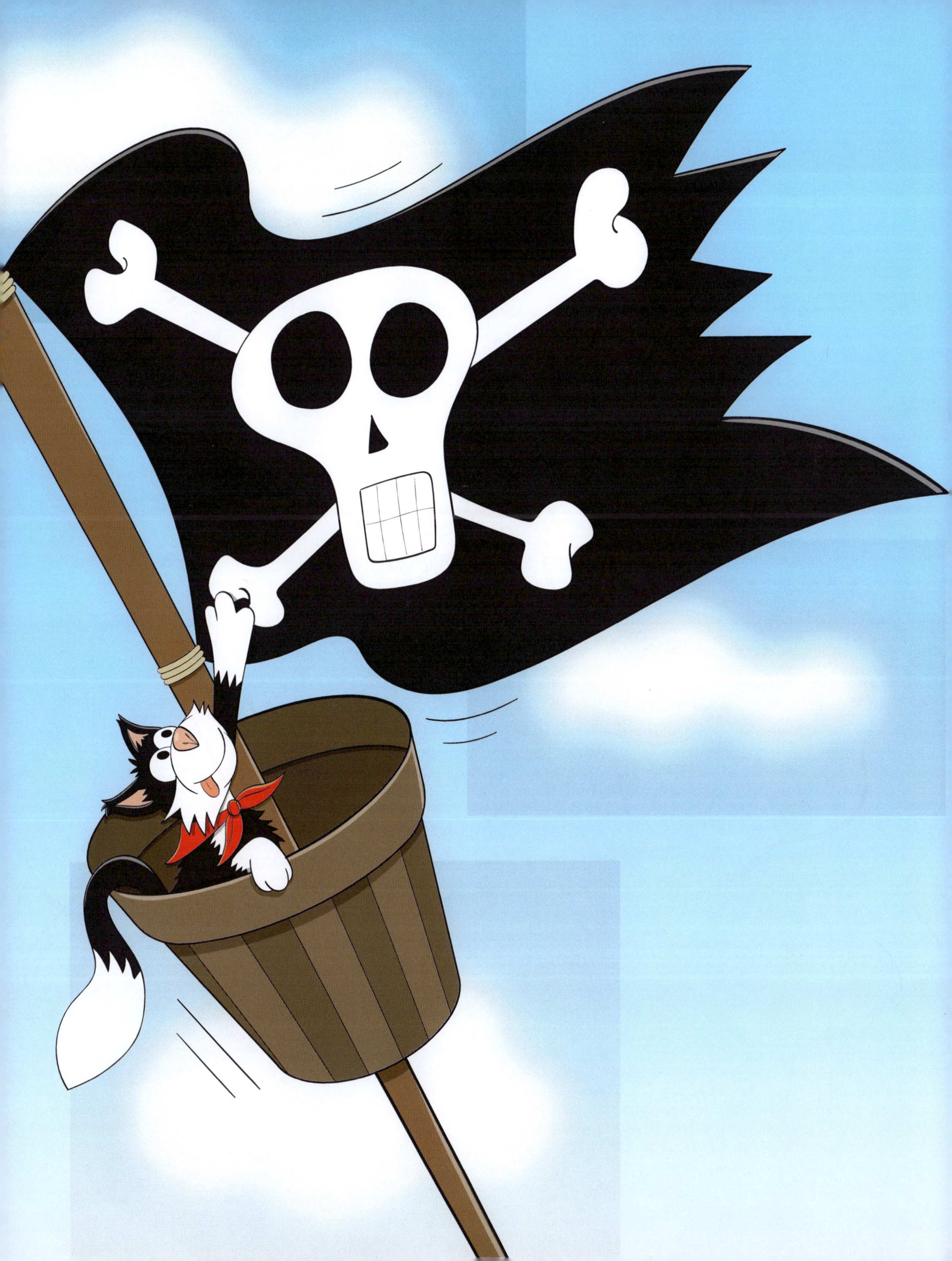

# Sharks!

*The Salty Dog* is beginning to sail through shark-infested waters and the crew peer nervously overboard, so they decide to sing a light-hearted song about sharks.

Out in the deep ocean, many sharks you will find
Some of them are nasty and some of them are kind
There are big ones and small ones and blue ones and grey
As long as it's just fish on their menu today...

### Chorus

Look out for the sharks in the...
Big, toothy sharks in the...
Hungry, great sharks in the sea...

The scariest, the mightiest, big shark who may bite
Is undoubtedly the one that they call 'The Great White'
Look out for the fin that sticks up in the air
And don't e'er go swimming nearby for a dare...

### Chorus

Great white sharks, great white sharks
They are so very real
Always looking out for a quick, easy meal
Great white sharks, great white sharks
They'll scare you to death
Or if not, they might kill you with their fishy bad breath...

### Chorus

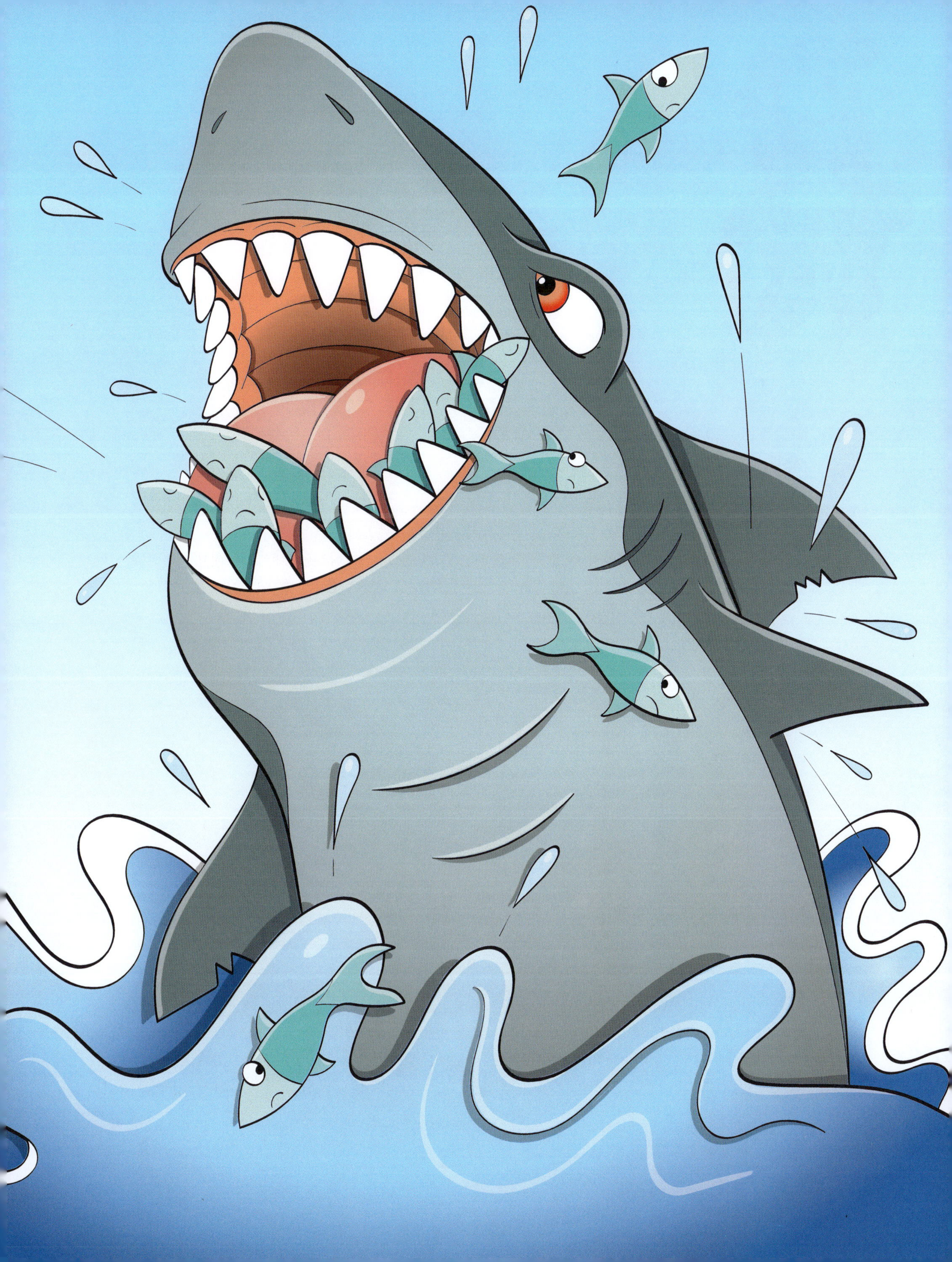

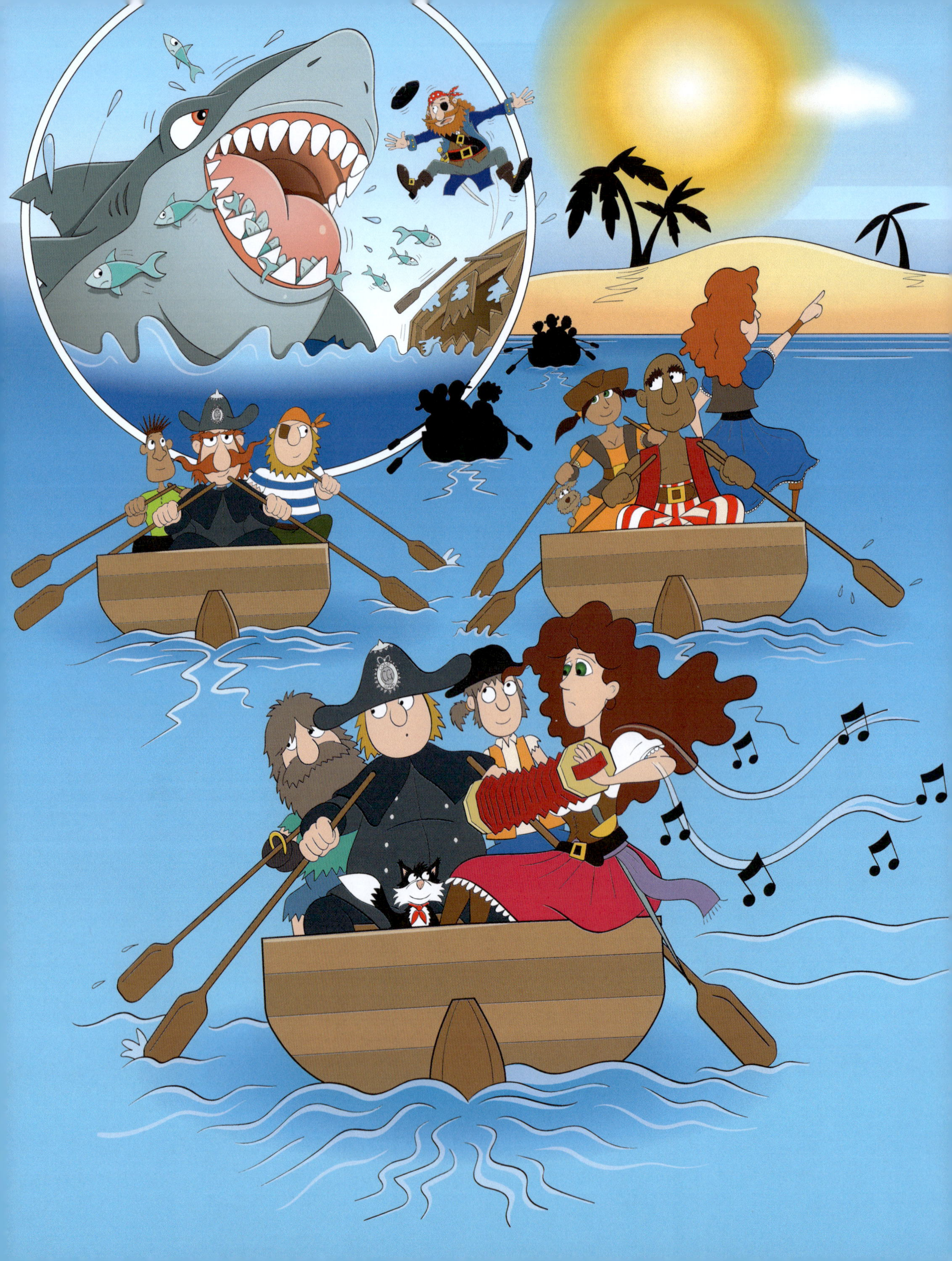

# Buried Treasure

Just as they spy the treasure isle in the distance, Captain Bligh jumps off his own plank into a small rowing boat, holding on to the treasure map, only to be gobbled up by a huge shark.

Bligh throws the map up; it floats up in the air and it gets tangled up in Rowena's long hair.

The members of the crew sense a ghostly presence pass by and they wonder if it be a farewell gesture from their former leader.

Rowena is strong and encourages the crew to carry on, so they anchor the ship in the bay and row over to the island, with the map to hand, believing that this will lead them to the buried treasure.

Yo ho! Heave ho! Yo ho! Heave ho!
We search for the buried treasure for which all of us would die
We follow the path on the treasure map from the ghost of Captain Bligh
But we must await 'til pieces-of-eight fulfil our hearts' desire
If there ain't no hitch, then we'll be rich and we can then retire...

Chorus

Yo ho! Heave ho! Yo ho!
Buried treasure (Yo ho!)
Buried treasure (Yo ho!)
Buried treasure...

Let's follow the moon as we shall be soon, the owners of starlit gold
In the hills to the west, there's a buried chest, or least 'tis what we're told
Full of gems and doubloons, them's pieces-of-eight, at last the trail is found
We're on the track, there's no turning back, there's treasure underground!

Chorus

We'll plod, plod, plod 'til we nod, nod, nod off into a deep, deep sleep
And sing, sing, sing for a jewel ring, oh one which we can keep
We'll dig, dig, dig 'til we jig, jig, jig, at the sight of precious, golden bars
Then we'll fight, fight, fight throughout the night, 'til we get what should be ours!

Chorus

CRANIUM COVE
Pirate Peaks
Octopus Pass
Cut Throat Caves
Dead Man Falls
Mermaid Lagoon
TREASURE
Strange Statues
Mayan

# Buried Treasure (Continued)

The bosun leads the crew, following the path outlined on the map and heads towards the spot marked with an X.

Rufus starts digging and unearths some stones until, finally, they find a large, wooden treasure chest. As they open the lid, trinkets, jewellery and a hoard of gold doubloons all spill out onto the sand.

HOORAY... HOORAY!!!

\*\*\*

Constable Crab turns traitor and threatens Bets, demanding they let him keep the treasure in exchange for her life.

Squawk comes to the rescue! He distracts Crab by pooping on his head, allowing Bets to push him over, then Rufus and Hilary attack him too.

Sergeant Rob ties up Crab, who is left to his own devices. He's marooned on the island, but there are enough resources here to survive alone.

# The Treasure Is Won

Back at the ship, they are all surprised to find that Captain Bligh had survived by wrestling the shark from inside and managing to swim out to safety.

Rowena is overjoyed and gives Bligh a big hug. Then they kiss each other.

He gets down on one knee and asks Rowena for her hand in marriage, to which she replies YES!

They set sail for home; the ship is laden with treasure. On the journey, there will be a happy wedding ceremony at sea, overseen by Bosun Bill.

A coastguard was naughty
and greedy too
A seagull did poop and our Rufus did chew
Bets gave him a push, Hilary dug in a claw
The traitor got all he was due
and some more...

Constable Crab backed down
and he threw up his arms
He said he was sorry,
no-one fell for his charms
The pirates joined up to condemn him so
He'll stay here behind
whilst the rest of us go

Chorus

The treasure is won (the traitor has lost)
The treasure is won (he's payin' the cost)
We've gold coming out of our ears
We're rich, so rich, we'll be rich
For the rest of our years,
the rest of our years

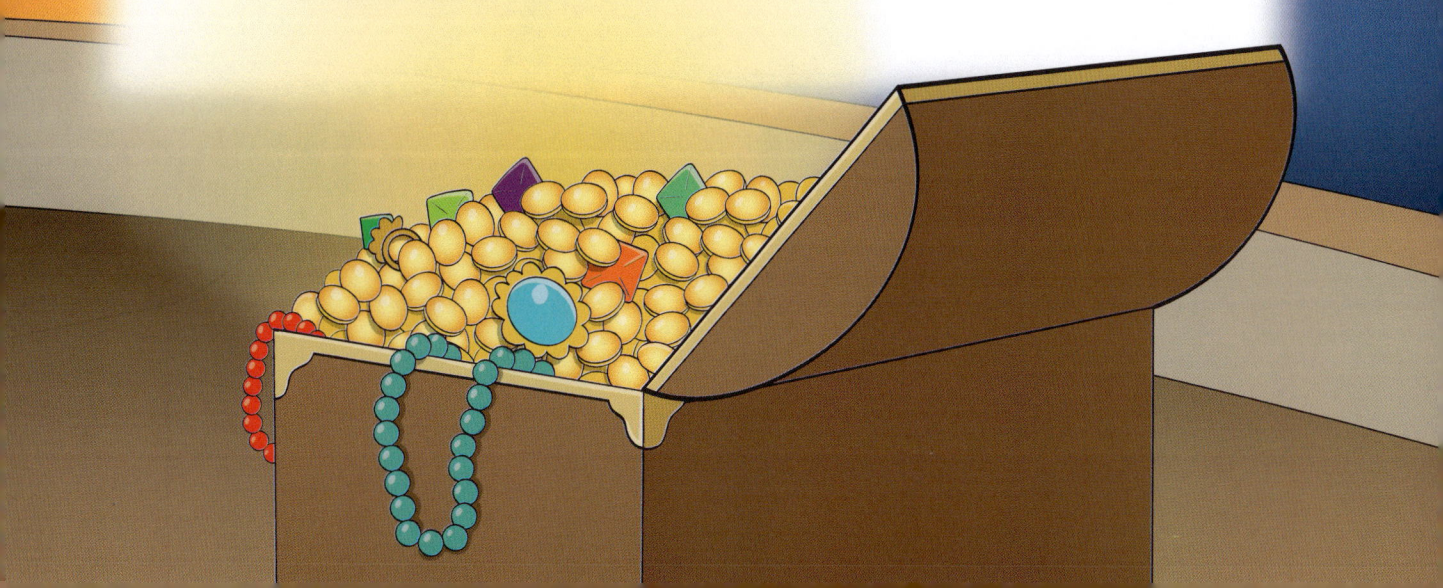

The traitor is left there
to fend for himself
He'll have to make do
without treasure for wealth
Our crew is so pleased, Cap'n Bligh is alive
And the bosun gives Roger
a happy 'high five'

Chorus

The treasure is won
(the traitor has run)
The treasure is won
(we're having some fun)
We've gold coming out of our ears
We're rich, so rich, we'll be rich
For the rest of our years,
the rest of our years

Our cap'n kneels down,
gives Rowena a ring
Rowena's so happy,
she just starts to sing
They both want a big pirate
wedding at sea
And this is for sure
what it's going to be...

Chorus

The treasure is won
(the traitor has failed)
The treasure is won
(his last ship has sailed)
We've gold coming out of our ears
We're rich, so rich, we'll be rich
For the rest of our years,
the rest of our years

# The Pirate Ship (Reprise)

ALL ABOARD! (All aboard)
For the pirate ship's in harbour
ALL ABOARD! (All aboard)
She's a-sailin' come the dawn
ALL ABOARD! (All aboard)
For the pirate ship's in harbour
She'll sail away through skies a-grey, with a pirate's cutlass drawn
With a pir-ate's cut-lass drawn…

## The End

# Also by Dave Whittle

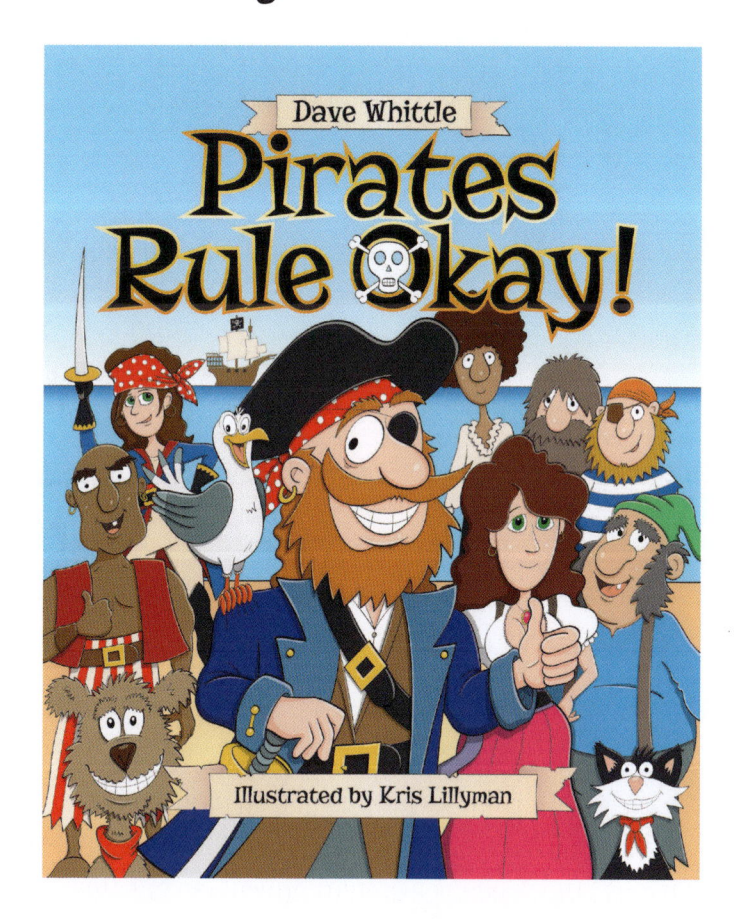

Check out www.piratesruleok.com for further details

Printed in Great Britain
by Amazon